Active Reviewing

A Practical Guide for Trainers and Facilitators

Table of Contents

Meet the authors –
and how the authors met!

About us ...

One day in the summer of 2014, Călin Iepure travelled to Bucharest in search of new ideas to use in his work as a trainer. Călin had signed up for a two day trainer-training workshop with me (Roger Greenaway). During this workshop he got very excited about how he could use these new ideas in his work as a trainer. He then shared these ideas with Bogdan Vaida (a fellow trainer from Timișoara) and they both started experimenting with these dynamic training techniques. Soon their colleagues started showing an interest and they decided to invite me to provide a workshop in Timișoara in the spring of 2015.

Over meals and coffee breaks, we started talking about making an online training course together. We quickly realised that in addition to our shared interest in making training more interactive, we each had a set of complementary skills: Călin's work with business start-ups and entrepreneurship; Bogdan's work with online training videos and my own niche providing training workshops in active reviewing skills and techniques.

... and a bit about the book

After launching our online course in the summer of 2015, we decided to create a book version of the online course. You may find that this book is all you need, but at some point you may decide that you would like to take a look at the more detailed online course.

I hope you find your journey into the world of active reviewing as rewarding as Călin found on his trip to the big city in the summer of 2014. On the next page, Bogdan takes over as the main narrator in your new book.
May your future participants enjoy the new opportunities that active reviewing opens up for them.
No more dull debriefs!

Dr. Roger Greenaway

Chapter 1: Why this book

If you want to help people learn from activities, exercises or experiences, this book is for you. This book fills a gap; it is the gap between doing an activity and learning from it. Plenty of books describe activities that are good for icebreaking, for team-building, for project management or for cross-cultural understanding, etc. A few of these books do give advice about reviewing (or debriefing) the activities, and 90% of the times it reads: "Here are some questions you can ask ...". How's that for boring and/or limiting?

The result of such advice is that reviews are often dull and they dwell on what went wrong. But why is that? Well, one of the reasons is because *the same* people speak up all the time. And that bores and might even annoy the rest of the participants. Thus, reviewing gets a bad name and people just want the review to finish as quickly as possible so that they can get on with the next activity.

This is a rare book for two reasons:
1. It is about reviewing (How many books have you come across on this subject?)
2. It is about reviewing *actively*.(Which makes it not just rare, but unique.)

With the help of this book, you can make reviews at least as engaging as the activities you are reviewing. No more discomfort. No more unwanted silences. No more superficial reviews. Just engaging and practical ways to help people learn from experience! How does that sound for a change?

Before we go any further, let's take a look at the conspicuous verb of the day- *to review.* The Free Dictionary.com has provided us with the following definition and of course, correct pronunciation:

"re·view (rĭ-vyoo′)

v. **re·viewed**, **re·view·ing**, **re·views**

v.tr.

1. To look over, study, or examine again: *reviewed last week's lesson.*

2. To consider retrospectively; look back on: *reviewed the day's events.*

3. To examine with an eye to criticism or correction: *reviewed the research findings.*

4. To write or give a critical report on (a new work or performance, for example).

Reading a definition already? My God, how boring! No, that's not the way to do it... Well, the truth is that reviewing can be all of these things you've read but at the same time, it CAN be a whole lot more. Reviewing is the key to learning from what happens; it gives you the opportunity to learn from mistakes and then build on what works well. Through reviewing you can explore mysteries, gain fresh insights and discover new possibilities!

Oh and then there is "Active Reviewing" ... this REALLY helps to ensure that reviewing is not just an intellectual exercise. It's far more dynamic because it involves thinking aloud with others, physical movement and communicating in ways that engage multiple senses and intelligences. Active reviewing uses and develops a broad range of learning skills. And at the end of it all, it also means testing out what you think you have learned ;)

Now, the word of the day here is "dynamic", so please highlight it. That is the key to understanding real, useful ways of reviewing. Also, if you want to find out how Archimedes came up with the whole "Eureka" business and how this will help you become a better trainer, don't stop here! Read on!

1.1: Eureka, Eureka !

Archimedes was a Greek scientist who lived in Syracuse nearly 200 years ago. Back then there was a certain King of the land and he wanted to wear a Golden Crown. (Quite fancy if you ask me...) So he gave some gold to a goldsmith to make a suitable crown. After a few days, the goldsmith brought the finished crown to the King. Naturally, the crown was weighed and it turned out that the weight of the crown was the same with the amount of gold given previously to the smith. Odd much? The King looked at the color of the crown and it too, arose suspicion. He thought that maybe the goldsmith had stolen some metal during the making of the crown. Consequently, he summoned his court scientist Archimedes and gave him the task of finding out the truth.

How did Archimedes do it? Well, the scientist thought about the problem day and night until one day... He was about to have his bath, but because he was too busy mulling over the task at hand, didn't notice that in the meantime, the bathtub had filled up with water. He just went into it and as a result, the water flowed over the brim of the bathtub. This whole incident gave him a brilliant idea and in his excitement he shouted "Eureka! Eureka!". Eureka in Greek means, "I have found it."

The Greek thinker had in fact discovered a physics law: different metals of the same weight have different volumes. Or in plain English- objects put in water will displace water...and the displaced water will be equal to their volume.

For example, an iron cube weighing a kilogram will disperse a certain amount of water. But an aluminum cube of the same weight will displace more water than the iron cube. Archimedes used this as the premise and thus, worked out a plan to find out the purity of the gold in the King's crown.

The Greek thinker took two bowls. He filled them with water to the brim. Then he placed each bowl separately in the middle of two large basins. He placed the crown in one bowl and saw that the water overflowed and had collected at the bottom of the outer bowl. Next step was to take a cube of pure gold. This cube of gold was equal in weight to the crown's and Archimedes proceeded with it in the same manner; he put this gold cube in the middle of the second bowl. Naturally, water overflowed (again!) and it got collected at the bottom of the bowl.

He determined the difference by comparing the water overflow from the two containers and came to the conclusion that the crown had poured out more water because it contained other metals beside gold. Archimedes reported his finding to the King who then confronted the goldsmith with solid proof. (Get it? Solid…. proof!) Of course, the smith confessed… he had indeed stolen some gold and added some other metals in the making. We never got the end of the story; most likely, the thief was beheaded. BUT we did get the "Eureka!" moment. Find out how this is valuable to you as a trainer in the next chapter!

1.2: Active Reviewing - drawing learning from experience

Reflecting is an experience

Archimedes' "Eureka!" moment while reflecting on the level of his bath water was accompanied by great excitement as he leapt from his bath to share his discovery with the world. Reflecting on experience can itself be a powerful experience. Receiving feedback about what you did and its consequences tends to be an emotionally charged experience for all involved – especially if it is about mistakes or failures. Receiving praise is quite an experience too – especially if it comes from several people at much the same time. An intense reflective dialogue while walking with a coach can be an emotional roller-coaster of a conversation. The best group reviews tend to be emotionally charged rather than being remote, distant and abstract. Reflection and learning have a strong emotional dimension. Only in rare circumstances should we try to strip out the emotion and treat reflection as a purely abstract process. We do not try stripping out the emotional content of poetry in order to understand it better: so why would we expect to understand experience any more by trying to put feelings to one side? Reflecting is an experience and trying to strip out the emotion is more likely to reduce its value than add to it.

'Active Reviewing' starts with an interest and commitment to learning from an experience. That is the 'reviewing' part of 'active reviewing'. The 'active' part emphasises the value of full engagement in the reviewing process. This means that everyone in the group is fully engaged. 'Active Reviewing' is a whole person approach that works on many levels, using movement and objects and images in ways that help people reflect and communicate while supporting each other's learning and development.

Roger says: *"It always seems a shame to see participants fully engaged in a team activity, only to see their attention and interest fade during an all-talk review. There is no reason why full engagement cannot continue throughout the whole process of learning from experience. This book provides you with a collection of Active Reviewing tools that will help you achieve high levels of engagement from your participants throughout the whole learning process."*

In the first part of the book you will learn what Active Reviewing actually is and how to get the learning experience you desire.

In the second part we will provide you with Active Reviewing methods to create engaging reflection experiences that people will never forget.

In the third part of the book we will look at how you can implement these methods into your trainings (when to do it, common traps you may be facing) and in that section we will also answer any question you may have about this field.

Fourth part deals with the future. Take the next step and maximize your learning experience.

And that's not it. Inside the book you'll find much much more; from simple principles learned through years of practice, down to tips & tricks for every specific method we present. Hungry for detail? Read on.

1.3: The practical, down-to-earth Active Reviewing Toolkit

If you'd like to receive The Active Reviewing Toolkit (a 32-page PDF detailing all the methods presented in the book with step-by- step instructions, useful variations and detailed explanations on why, how and when to use them), free book updates and other complementary materials, subscribe here: http://www.activereviewing.com/bonuses ! You'll get all the bonuses on your email address, fast and easy!

1.4 Facilitator, Trainer or Public Speaker?

"I HEAR AND I FORGET. I SEE AND I REMEMBER. I DO AND I UNEDRSTAND." - Confucius
Nowadays, more and more companies and organziations have realised how important their employee participation to specialized courses is. In a hyper-competitive world, in a world where people make the difference, companies are increasingly focusing on developing their staff's knowledge and know-how.
The first advantage of taking part in educational programmes within your company is increased productivity which consequently limits the number of errors (human errors, that is) in general. Another one is that these trainings have become the new criteria for what makes an organization successful. So you have to ask youself- go for mediocrity or go for more, for better?

Although the market is quite responsive to the employees' learning needs, there is rarely a clear distinction between a Facilitator, a Trainer or a Public Speaker. They do have common points, but their teaching styles differ substantially from context to context.

The test below will help you identify your strengths and establish your current teaching style- the right one, the right way:

Test: Are you a Facilitator, a Trainer or a Public Speaker?

Tick the box with the most suitable affirmation for you. Give yourself 0 points if you tick the box under "Never", 1 point if you answer "Sometimes", 2 points if you associate your answer to "Often" and 3 points if you go for "Always".

No	Affirmation	Never	Some times	Often	Always
1	When I'm in front of an audiance, I like to be heard				
2	I use different tools in my teaching				
3	I feel more comfortable				

	with a group of under 20 people				
4	I don't like being in the spotlight				
5	I inspire and motivate others when I speak				
6	I like doing demonstrations				
7	I like telling stories and/or funny tales				
8	I like mingling at events				
9	My trainees should implement what they are taught				
10	First I analyze my client's needs and then I recommend a programme that will fill in existing gaps				
11	I like helping people learn from their experiences				
12	I think interaction can make a difference in the trainings I do				

13	I'm careful how I communicate nonverbally				
14	My dialogues are balanced				
15	I make handouts for my trainings				
16	I focus on content				
17	I like to have individual chats with my trainees				
18	I focus on process				
19	I like it when people applaud me and my course				
20	I believe that I could be a good coach				

At the end, sum up the points to see what your current style tends towards.

STYLE	SPEAKER		TRAINER		FACILITATOR	
	Affirmation	Answer	Affirmation	Answer	Affirmation	Answer

AFFIRMATION	1		3		2	
	5		6		4	
	7		10		9	
	8		14		11	
	13		15		12	
	16		16		18	
	19		17		20	
TOTAL						

As you've seen from the test, a facilitator or a trainer is not a public speaker! Just as a trainer or a facilitator is not necessarily a person who delivers information; in fact, to pass on information is just a small part of the job!

While a public speaker's role is to inform, a trainer spends between 20 and 40% of their time delivering information and the rest of the time, he or she focuses on how to apply abstract information and interact with participants. A facilitator's main concern is creating context and guiding the learning process.

So, according to the way a message is conveyed, these people's behaviour shows noticeable distinctions: *a public speaker talks in front of an audiance, a trainer interacts with the audiance* and *a facilitator sets the scene* so that interaction with the audiance can later be made.

When it comes to the segment of the message itself, a public speaker passes on pre-researched and pre-learned information- you could say that they know what to say by heart-, whereas a trainer will repeatedly ask participants about their needs, tiressly trying to figure out what else they need to learn and focusing on gap-filling. And last but not least, a facilitator is the one who determines their needs and extracts the missing information directly from the trainees.

A public speaker's main tools are humor and stories; a trainer or facilitator has other aces up their sleeves. The first is more appropriate for short term motivation; a public speaker will be able to keep it going during conferences and brief courses. A trainer, on the other hand, has the ability to engage participants in longer trainings. A facilitator shines brightest when is given the chance to guide the development of a group in the desired direction.

Below you have a table that explains the differences more clearly:

	SPEAKER	TRAINER	FACILITATOR
ROLE/PURPOSE	Informs Convinces	Develops abilities that can later turn into habits	Facilitates learning and skill Guides the

	Inspires Entertains	Alters behaviour	learning process
STYLE	Usually, a one-way communication	2-way communication (dialogue)	Group communication (group chat)
METHODS	Telling	Determines what participants already know Determines what they need to learn Fills in gaps	Determines goals Creates context Guides the learning process
TOOLS	Humor Stories Visual aids	Presentation Role-Play Exercices Case studies Demonstrations Visual	Questions Feedback Guided experience Role-Play Debriefing Chairing Brainstorming Coaching Other educational

		elements Questions	tools
EVALUATION/ ASSESSMENT	Applaude	The degree of behavioural change	The extent to which new skills have been integrated
PROGRAMME	Open courses (Short) Conferences	Long and open courses Trainings Workshops	Long open courses Workshops Teambuildings Consulting (sometimes)

Now that you've found out what the differences between the 3 main styles are, I invite you to answer the next 3 questions:
1. What is my main style?
2. What will I use in the future in order to develop my facilitation style?
3. Which top 3 facilitation tools will I use in the future to provide a unique/unforgettable experience?

Chapter 2: ART: The Active Reviewing Toolkit

2.1: Reviewing with playing cards - a practical model

The first model I'll be describing is called ART which stands for Active Reviewing Toolkit. This is a practical and visual way to pinpoint the needs of your trainee or your group. You will need 4 cards, used in the following sequence- 1st. Diamond (facts), 2nd. Heart (feelings and intuition), 3rd. Spade (findings) and 4th.Club (futures)- and an extra one card, The Joker. The Joker in the centre represents <u>freedom</u> and <u>flexibility</u>.

Next, you are provided with in-depth descriptions and explanations of the roles the cards take on.

1. The **Joker** is the blank or wild card that can mean anything you want it to. The Joker is here for a serious reason. It reminds us not to mistake the model for reality. It's very important to know that models only simplify reality; they don't identify with it. Look at the Joker as a way to escape from the restrictions of a model- we might say it keeps us alert to exceptions. So basically, you have the freedom to experiment within and beyond the given model.

2. The **Diamond** represents the experience as it is perceived in that very moment: both a mixture of facts and impressions. This card has some unique characteristics, highlighted by keywords. Firstly, <u>its *sparkle* catches our attention.</u> Ask yourself: what do you first notice, perceive or assume about the experience? Secondly, <u>the diamond has *many sides.*</u> Imagine it rotating in your mind; can you say what it looks like from other perspectives? Now think about how others might perceive the same object. And thirdly, <u>the diamond is a *valuable* resource.</u> The question remains: How can you, the trainer draw value from it?

3. The **Heart** also represents the experience, but focuses more on the feelings and emotions it generates. The following questions are quite important: What emotions and intuitions are found within the experience? What was it like? Did it remind you of another experience? How was it similar or different? How intense was it? These questions will help the participants bond because they'll find common ground, discover similar tastes and raise their empathy.

The **red cards** (diamonds and hearts) together represent the story of the experience. This story describes the version of events from which learning and development will be derived through further reflection and analysis. The red cards give substance to the story, which is already a useful process.

4. Now let's look at the black cards! The **Spade** digs deeper because that it involves examining the story. Here, questions seeking reason, explanation, and the

formulation of conclusions are relevant. Examples: *Why did it turn out like that? What made you think that? What can we learn from this? What are we finding out? What other explanations are possible?* And so on.

5. The **Club** represents future growth - in many possible directions. These might include action plans, predictions, making decisions, imagining and even dreaming. Ask yourself, *how can we best take our learning into the future? What can you learn from past actions?*

The **black cards** (spades and clubs) together represent the various ways in which people can learn from their experiences and take their learning forwards. The red cards represent the story while the black cards represent learning, change and growth. Black cards are about the story's significance and making a difference.

In a nutshell:
- Facts are represented by diamonds.
- Feelings are represented by hearts.
- Findings are represented by spades.
- And future outcomes are represented by clubs.

Moving on, the basic sequence you have to remember is: Facts -> Feelings -> Findings-> Futures. And The Joker, well, this is a wild card that can be used at any given moment.

The material that follows is structured using this model. You will receive the tools you need to identify facts, reveal feelings, dig deeper and inspire action.

But watch out! If you simply use this cycle as a guide for sequencing your questions, you will <u>not</u> be entering the world of *active* reviewing. And in a short while the pattern of your questions will become predictable and boring.

<u>A recommendation to make things fun and interesting:</u>

If you think "Diamonds - Facts - Action Replay" and ask participants to re-enact key incidents, then you will be definitely getting the keys to the castle and unlocking all the benefits the method has to offer!

If you think "Hearts - Feelings - Empathy Test", we can give a 99% guarantee that your participants will be fully engaged in sharing their feelings within a minute.

If you think "Spades - Findings - Horseshoe", participants will instantly be on their feet and talking about "reasons why" with their "friendly neighbours". And if you think "Clubs - Futures - Back to the Future", then everyone will be building up each other's confidence for their next steps on the journey towards their goal". These are all physical exercises that promote participation, reflection and learning: very, very different to asking questions to the whole group.

Although Active Reviewing often includes the asking of questions, it is *never just* the asking of questions.

And the Joker (representing freedom and flexibility) is never far away!)

Quiz: Reviewing with playing cards

1. Fill in the blanks

Facts are represented by _____.

_____ are represented by hearts.

Findings are represented by _____.

_____ are represented by clubs.

Freedom and flexibility are represented by the

_____.

2. True or false:

Using active reviewing techniques associated with the red suits will generally help to enhance the quality of stories that people tell about their experiences.

True

False

3. Active reviewing techniques associated with Spades will help participants find meaning, understanding, explanations and new insights.

True

False

4. Which of these questions is least likely to belong with the club card?

    a. What you were doing at that moment?

    b. Can you show me how you would begin the task if you were to have a second chance?

    c. Would you please make a plan that shows the steps you will take to achieve your goal?

    d. Referring only to events during the course so far, what are your 3 top reasons for why you should be chosen to lead the next project?

    e. Would you please find an object or picture that represents a goal that you would really like to achieve?

5. What does the Joker Card represent?

a. Fun
b. Freedom
c. An open question
d. What comes after 'Futures'

(you can find the answers in the Appendix)

2.2: ♦ *Facts: Activity Map*

The Activity Map is a map with four areas on which reveals the activities that participants like and dislike.The group version involves marking the areas on the floor.

There is a lot you can do with activity maps; they can represent the starting point for discussions, which if sustained, will readily bring out a person's values and principles behind their choices. It is a quick way for people to get to know each other better.

Therefore, The Activity Maps can be used for:
- Participants to introduce themselves,
- Pairs to get to know each other well,
- Appreciating the different ways in which activities can be of value,
- Identifying changes at the end of a course,
- Discussing values and principles underlying activity preferences.

I'd like to try	I don't want to try
1. Activity Map 2. Horseshoe 3. Games!!	1. Football 2. 3.
I enjoy	I didn't enjoy
1. Storyline 2. Goal Keepers 3. Action Replay	1. 2. 3.

How to make the map

First, you the trainer must explain that the map is for their own personal record as well as for showing to others. Each person draws four squares (as shown in the image) and lists at least three activities in each square. You can start by limiting this exercise to activities you've included in your course curriculum. Then, continue by asking people to add up to three more activities in each square - from any part of their life. If individuals end up with one or two blank squares - that's OK. Blank squares can communicate a lot!

How to share the map between each other

1. Your trainees find a partner and talk through each other's maps. Then they discuss any surprises they may find.

2. In small groups of 3, they look for similarities and differences.
3. In the whole group, each person chooses one activity from each of their squares and shares with the group (adding short explanations if they want to).

A recommendation: near the end of a course, you can ask participants to take another look at their maps and then make changes using arrows. You are hoping for positive changes. But inviting people to share disappointments (if any) may help to turn negatives into positives.

As a game

The Activity Map can also be used as a game, using two ropes and four labelled cards.
With the cards, mark out four zones on the ground corresponding to the four areas of the map.
Then, with the ropes, mark the lines that separate the four areas - as shown in the image.

FUTURE

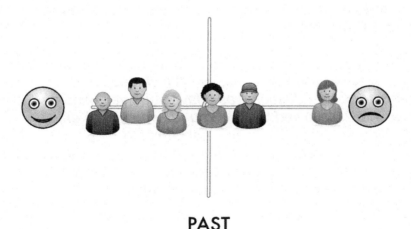

PAST

Call out the name of an activity and ask everyone to go to the area where that activity would belong on their own personal map. The happy-sad line can be used as a spectrum. If outside, use a slope with happy uphill and sad lower down.

Keep calling out activities, pausing now and again for comments and questions.

And to make it more of a game, you can let participants call out the names of the activities. See what kind of things your students are drawn to and to which they are not. One of the best things about this method is that you can correct any false assumptions, allay concerns or offer extra support if appropriate.

Not every trainer has absolute flexibility when it comes to what and how to teach the course, but including The Activity Map (even in its shorter, 15-minute version) will definitely catch your audience's attention.

The Activity Map belongs near the beginning of a course when discussing what lies ahead. But what if can you replay an experience? Would you be interested in that? The next chapter, Action Replay offers just that!

Roger says: *I once used Activity Map with a group of environmental educators, which included some hunters. My question was "Have you ever killed an animal?" followed by "Did you (or would you) enjoy killing an animal?". As you can imagine, these questions went much further than likes and dislikes and went straight into core values - even though hunting was not part of the programme.*

2.3: ♦ Facts: Action Replay

Action Replay is a method best suited to the debriefing of exercises in which there is plenty of action involving the whole group. If the 'action' was repetitive, it may be too difficult for participants to synchronise their replay. Games that involve getting the whole group from A to B are often well suited, while mental puzzles or board games are less suitable.

For the activity, you need a dummy microphone and a dummy remote control. You'll be taking some interviews :)

Action Replay involves re-enacting an activity as if a video of the activity is being replayed. Just as on TV, the action is played back to examine an incident more closely or to replay an event worth celebrating. In this age full of TV and video, the exercise is readily understood and needs little explanation.

Compared to video work, Action Replay is much quicker to set up, edit and replay because there are no technical problems!

How to use the props

> The Dummy Microphone

A dummy microphone adds extra purpose (and interest) to the replay. Any group member (actor or audience) can pause the action and pick up the dummy microphone to interview someone involved in the action. They can ask questions from any point of the learning cycle:

- To clarify what had been going on up to that point,
- To give people a chance to express their feelings (especially if unknown to others),
- To analyse the situation (Why were you doing that? How did that happen?),
- Or to look to the future (How could you build on what worked well? What could you take from this experience into the workplace?).

>The Dummy Remote Control

As an alternative, you can introduce a dummy remote control before the replay starts. You (or the participants) can preselect which moments to replay by requesting 'Selected Highlights' or you can just ask for the whole activity to be replayed. While taking part in a replay anyone can ask for the remote to slow down the replay at a particular moment or to see it again. Remind people about useful buttons on the remote and warn that you may invent some new buttons that no one has ever heard of before. Once you have demonstrated the possibilities of using the remote control, participants can take it in turns to direct the action. The dummy controls are not only fun to play with, they also provide opportunities for some very focused and controlled debriefing. Action Replay is also readily adapted for rehearsing future scenarios.

As you can see, the method has quite a few advantages:
- It is more convenient and versatile - so it can be used almost anywhere;
- It keeps involvement and energy high;
- It is an exercise in memory, creativity, and teamwork;
- It provides opportunities for leadership, interviewing and commentating;
- And it can be used as a search technique to find incidents or issues to debrief more thoroughly.

.

A few words from Roger's experience: *I first learned about Action Replay when working young people who had been caught stealing from shops. I would encourage them to pause the replay whenever they could see a way of acting differently and staying out of trouble. Through this method they were learning - and practising - how to resist negative peer pressure and stand up for themselves. Many years later it was Hector (a karaoke fan and facilitator) who added the dummy microphone to the process - making it an even more versatile technique.*

Quiz: Working with facts and first assumptions

1. Which is the most unlikely outcome as a result of using Activity Map?
   a. Activity Map can serve as an appetiser for the course ahead - if you include activities that are part of the course.
   b. Activity Map can give you early warning about how you may want to adjust your approach.
   c. Activity Map can result in participants learning about each other's likes, dislikes and values.
   d. Activity Map leads to participants appreciating the different ways in which activities can be of value.
   e. Activity Map can result in participants developing their confidence in map making.

2. The Activity Map belongs near the beginning of a course when discussing what lies ahead.
True
False

3. Action Replay is best suited to the debriefing of exercises in which there is plenty of action involving the whole group.
True
False

4. Which of these benefits is least likely to result from using Action Replay?
Action Replay keeps involvement and energy high.
Action Replay builds confidence in participants' performing abilities.
Action Replay can create useful video to assist with learning transfer.
Through Action Replay participants come to understand more about why others behaved as they did.

Action Replay may reveal incidents or issues that are worth debriefing more thoroughly.

5. A _____ microphone adds extra purpose (and interest) to the replay. Any group member (actor or audience) can _____ the action and pick up the dummy microphone to _____ someone involved in the action. They can ask questions from any stage of the 4F learning _____.

(you can find the answers in the Appendix)

2.4: ♥ Feelings: Empathy Test - how would your partner answer this question?

In this chapter you will be given an empathy tool which you can use to get your students to share without being invasive or without pressuring them into telling personal stories. Roger says: *Empathy Test is so much better than a general check-in to the whole group asking about people's feelings, energy levels, relevance, confidence etc. - because in Empathy Test you can see all this information at a glance, while participants are having fun, getting to know each other and are talking about the topic in your question.*

Empathy Test involves putting yourself in your partner's shoes and guessing how they would respond.
It is best used after a paired exercise. Just ask pairs to find a space on their own (within earshot of the trainer) and to stand back to back. Each person guesses their partner's answer by guessing the height of their partner's hand.

This is a fun game that develops empathy between pairs. Basically, partners guess each other's answers using a hand height scale (raising and lowering their hand to what they think their partner's hand position is). To implement it, ask participants to stand back to back with their partner and to quickly choose who is A and who is B.

Ask A's to take a half metre step forwards to create a small space between partners.

All A's answer your first scalable question by hand height.

B's guess the level of A's hand by their own hand level.

Then, tell them to turn around and voila!

Next question is for B to answer – with A's guessing B's answer and so on.

It takes around 30 seconds per question plus a 30 seconds chat, in pairs, after each revelation.

The exercise works best after any paired activities or after any linear activities where people move in a line or wait turns in a queue.

When used after activities where pairs interact in some way; you will probably see an increase in team spirit. And you will certainly see an increase in empathy.

Variations:

1. Questions don't have to be about feelings - although that is a good place to start. You can ask anything guessable on a scale.
2. You can use random partners (though it's more difficult and results in less successful guessing)
3. Head height rather than hand height (it's more fun, but less accurate).
4. Giving an overall score to partner on the closeness of their guessing.

5. Guessers can close their eyes while they guess.

On the plus part: you'll hear all the buzz and laughter when they first turn around.
And on the minus: it doesn't work if partners did not notice each other during the event that your Empathy Test questions refer to.
Tip: use plenty of space so that each pair can focus on each other without being too distracted by what others are doing or saying.

You can download the Active Reviewing Toolkit to find out how to implement Empathy Test with storytelling and also get some sample questions at http://www.activereviewing.com/bonuses .

2.5: ♥ Feelings: Storyline

People talk quite naturally of their 'highs and lows' being 'as high as a kite' or 'down in the dumps'. A Storyline is a timeline showing these fluctuations.
*   It's a chart made by participants showing their 'ups and downs' over a period of time.
*   The chart can represent a 'journey' through an online course, a work project or while learning a skill.
*   Storyline can chart anything that fluctuates such as emotion, involvement, motivation, effort or difficulty.
*   Usually charting the 'journey' makes it easier for speakers to communicate.
*   It also makes it easier for others to see the big picture, follow the story and ask good questions.

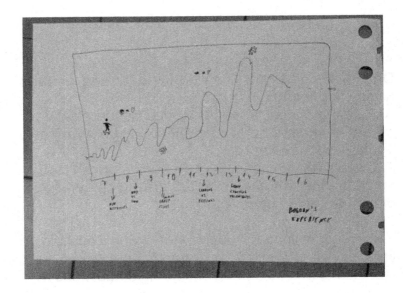

So what will you gain by using Storyline? It will...

- provide thinking and preparation time before people tell their 'story'.
- help people focus on a particular theme while telling of their story (e.g. involvement, understanding, relevance, confidence, performance...).
- help participants notice similarities and differences in each other's stories.
- stimulate interest, empathy and support between participants.
- provide insights into what motivates or demotivates each participant.
- bring out stories of resilience – if asked, "What helped you recover from the dips?"

Because you don't want the setup to eat up valuable time, here are some guidelines:

- For making individual Storylines, each participant needs pen and paper.

- For a more active version, you need to provide participants with 5 metre ropes for charting their story on the floor.
- You can also do this in pairs and if ropes or space are limited, participants can tell their stories one at a time.
- To go beyond storytelling and encourage the analysis and discussion of the stories, you will need a good supply of suitable questions.

Let me give you some sample questions that stimulate reflections about a storyline that is focused on feelings:

1. Can you name five emotions that you were feeling at different points in your story?
2. What caused your high points? How did you (or others) contribute to these high points?
3. What did you or others do to help you bounce back from your low points?
4. How did your feelings influence what you said or did?
5. In a similar situation in future, how would you like your Storyline to be different?

For pluses, minuses, tips, things to watch out for and many more, don't forget to download the additional material at http://www.activereviewing.com/bonuses .

Roger says: *I first came across this method as a multicoloured chart on a wall. It looked very pretty but it took ages to make and it didn't seem very time effective. I started using the rope version after rock climbing sessions (when pen and paper were not handy) and I now generally prefer the rope version after any activity because walking along the rope really brings out people's storytelling skills.*

Quiz: Focusing on feelings and experiences

1. Which of these statements does not apply to Empathy Test?
Empathy Test can be useful for Training Needs Analysis
Empathy Test questions don't have to be about feelings.
Empathy Test involves metaphorically "walking in the other person's shoes".
Empathy Test is a fun game that develops empathy between pairs.
Empathy Test works best after paired activities or after activities where people move in a line or wait turns in a queue.
2. In Empathy Test it is quite easy for the facilitator to briefly scan the whole group to see how they are responding to each question.
True
False
3. Storyline has many applications including: serving as a record of a personal journey through a course of study, or showing ups and downs during a new challenge at work or while persevering with learning a skill.
True
False
4. Which of these statements misrepresents Storyline?
Storyline is a chart made by participants showing their 'ups and downs' over a period of time.
Storyline can chart anything that fluctuates such as emotion, involvement, motivation, effort or difficulty.

Storyline works best for people who have high emotional intelligence.
Storyline provides preparation time and a visual aid that makes it easier for speakers to communicate.
Storyline stimulates interest, empathy and support between participants.
5. Storyline can provide insights into what motivates or demotivates each participant.
True
False

(you can find the answers in the Appendix)

2.6: ♠ *Findings: Goal Keepers - how am I doing?*

Goal Keepers is an experiential method and what it does is integrate feedback and review into the activity, instead of having to wait for the post-activity review (when the opportunity for timely feedback has passed by). In this exercise pairs pay special attention to each other's goals (or objectives) and so they become their partner's "goal keeper".

This is a fairly unobtrusive way of reminding individuals of their goals or action points during an activity.
Each individual chooses up to three personal goals (or action points) arising from a recent review. Examples are: 'I should speak up more', 'listen more' or 'not give up easily'.

Each person writes down each goal on a card. The cards are given to a team of observers. Ideally, you split your group in 2, one half observes the other half in action. During the activity, observers look out for individuals who do not appear to be implementing their action points and then, quietly show the card corresponding to the objective each participant had written down earlier.

Any disputes about this feedback are postponed until the review.

For an in-depth understanding of the process, follow these steps:

1. Each person declares three objectives or goals to a partner. These goals describe what that person wants to pay special attention to during the activity.
2. Each goal is shortened to a key word or key phrase and each goal is noted in bold letters on a separate card.
3. Partners exchange cards.
4. The group is split into "observers"and "doers". During the group activity partners alternate roles; more precisely, they do that every 5 minutes.
5. Feedback is given non-verbally by the 'observer' during the exercise. The observer (who is the 'goal keeper' for their partner's goals) shows a relevant card and provides a thumb signal. Thumb down means "pay more attention to what it says on the card" while thumb up signals that "you are doing this well".

6. When swapping roles provide time for paired conversations. Ideally, such conversations are led by the 'doers'. This avoids the risk that the observers (the 'goal keepers') give unwanted observations and opinions. The opportunity to have these conversations allows for more sensitivity and understanding than is possible when making silent gestures as a goal keeper.

The obvious benefit here is instant feedback! This exercise works wonders in activities where individuals are so immersed in the action they forget they have something to improve.

I (your friendly narrative voice, Bogdan) am using a variation of this exercise in my public speaking trainings. When I see a participant with a bad posture, I select 2 "angels" to stand behind the participant while he or she is delivering a presentation. Each time he or she slouches, the angels touch the participant's shoulder, delivering a stimulus that reminds the participant to maintain proper posture. After a few touches, the participant manages to remember to maintain the posture on their own.

Roger says: *Goal Keepers came from an assignment I was given as part of a train-the-trainer programme. The challenge was to develop a way of speeding up learning. I used to call it 'Jogger Cards' but this referred to the materials. So I now prefer to call it 'Goal Keepers' because this title refers to the observer and to the responsibilities shared by both the observer and the doer.*

2.7: ♠ Findings: Horseshoe

Horseshoe is a scaling exercise in which participants show their attitude towards an issue. Horseshoe kickstarts group discussion by making each person's point of view visible and (optionally) by giving everyone preparation time by first speaking with a 'friendly neighbour'.

This reviewing method is a variation of a technique that goes under many names including: 'spectrum', 'line-up', 'positions', 'diagonals' and 'silent statements'. The main difference is that these other methods use straight lines, whereas the 'horseshoe' is a curved line. In this method, you simply define the two ends of the spectrum and ask everyone to stand at a point on the line that represents their point of view.

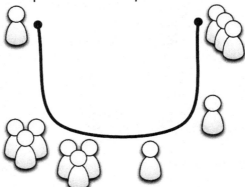

Let me provide an example: On the spectrum, one end represents "We were a pretty good team during that exercise", and the other end says "We were a hopeless team during that exercise". Everyone chooses their point on the line and then talks to one or two neighbors to check whether they need to adjust their own position on the line. Once everyone is in position, you can encourage questions from participants to each other. Everyone should have a chance to explain their position, after which everyone should have a chance to move to show whether or not their views on the issue have changed.

The friendly neighbour part of the process is particularly useful when working with large groups where there is not sufficient time or interest to hear from each individual. Its primary value is that it gives everyone an instant opportunity to speak even if only to one or two people. It can also be a useful final stage to help people reflect with a partner on the group discussion.

So what are the benefits?
Well…
- When standing in a curve, everyone is more likely to be in eye contact with each other - which makes facilitating whole group discussion much easier,
- You quickly discover the range of opinions on an issue,
- You also create a platform for group discussion in which participants naturally show an interest in each other's chosen positions,
- Besides all of this, you can bring rarely heard voices into your group discussion, usually belonging to reflective people.

I recommend the following **variation for more movement:** It may be helpful to ask different questions during the Horseshoe activity, like for instance:. "How would you each have rated this team before the exercise started?" "What was the quality of teamwork like up to the end of the initial planning?" or "What is your personal prediction for the quality of teamwork in the next exercise?".

There is also a **variation for more comfort**: Arrange chairs in the shape of a horseshoe with the facilitator sitting in the gap. Have about twice as many chairs as there are people to make movement easier and to allow for different patterns of clusters and spaces to develop.

For trainers who'd like to go the extra mile, I suggest a **variation for more depth**: Use this tool to explore moral issues or company values as well as for reviewing group exercises.

I've personally used this technique in a public speaking training where I've asked people if they preferred more experiential games or more theory. You can guess their responses.

I invite you to try this technique in your trainings and to write your experience in the comments section. How did the participants react? Did you use a variation of the technique? Invented a new way to use it?

From Roger's experience: *I wonder if you have ever asked a group to raise their hands if they agree with something that you have said? Well – Horseshoe is a great alternative because it brings out shades of opinion. When I first came across this method it was a straight line method. It was a spectrum in which each person would choose their place to stand on a straight spectrum. But this didn't allow for a good group discussion because you couldn't all see each other's position on the spectrum. So what I did with this method was to bend the line around into almost a circle (or horseshoe shape) so that everyone could see everyone else. I also like to include the "friendly neighbour" process because it guarantees that everyone is participating right from the very beginning of the process. So instead of 'hands up' try this 'stand up' process – if you want thoughtful participation from everyone.*

Quiz: Digging deeper and finding out

1. The purpose of Goal Keepers is to build participants' confidence by helping them create an impenetrable defence system.
True
False

2. The purpose of Goal Keepers is to generate instant feedback during an activity and so accelerate the process of learning by doing.
True
False

3. Horseshoe is a variation of a technique that goes under many names including: 'spectrum', 'line-up', 'positions', 'diagonals' and 'silent _____'. The main difference is that these other methods use _____ lines, whereas the 'horseshoe' is a _____ line. In this method, you simply define the two ends of the spectrum and ask everyone to _____ at a point on the line that represents their point of view. The benefit of the horseshoe shape is that everyone is more likely to be in _____ contact with each other - which makes _____ whole group discussion much easier.

4. Which is the least likely benefit to arise from using Horseshoe?
You quickly discover the range of opinions on an issue.
Participants naturally show an interest in each other's chosen positions.

Participants readily find allies during the friendly neighbour part of the process.

You can readily assess participants by observing the positions they choose.

Participants who need time to reflect are better prepared for joining in the group discussion.

5. Horseshoe provides a useful structure for exploring moral issues or company values as well as for reviewing group exercises.

True

False

(you can find the answers in the Appendix)

2.8: ♣ Futures: Back to the Future - using your assets to help you achieve your goals

Thinking about results is forward thinking. But what if backward thinking could help people get the results they want? Asking people about what they already have is a good preparation. And why not, it can even help them find shortcuts, time-savers and forgotten resources.

Back to the Future is a short journey for two people in which one person is the 'coach', and the other is the 'traveller'. Several pairs can work together as coach and traveller at the same time. Allow time for participants to swap roles and repeat the exercise – so that everyone can experience both roles.

The method is a 'just-in-time' review process that precedes planning. Think of it as an audit of assets, strengths and resources. It is not a substitute for making a plan - but it is likely to result in a much better plan.

Setup

The 'traveller' places on the floor a word, symbol or picture that represents their goal and explains it to their 'coach'.
Both walk about 5 metres away - optionally laying down a rope to mark out the journey.
The 'traveller' faces away from their goal and towards their 'coach' – check the illustration.

GOAL

Traveller

What past experiences will help you achieve your goal?

Coach

The 'coach' asks what they already have that will help them on their journey.

Whenever the 'traveller' states a helpful factor they take a step backwards towards their goal. Large steps indicate very helpful factors; small steps indicate slightly helpful factors.

It is the traveller who decides how large the steps should be.

Here are some useful questions to ask the traveller:

- 'What knowledge and experience do you have that will help you on this journey?'
- 'What values and motivations do you have that will help you on this journey?'
- 'What resources and support do you have that will help you on this journey?'

No need to write them down, these and some other questions, are written in the additional material.

Roadblocks? The 'coach' can apply the same questioning process to any problem that the 'traveller' happens to mention: *"What ... do you already have that will help you overcome this obstacle?"*

Why does this method work?

As I've said in the beginning of the subchapter, asking people about assets they already have helps them find shortcuts, time-savers and forgotten resources. The exercise involves recalling relevant experiences and drawing confidence, energy and learning from them.

Back to the Future helps people approach their goal more wisely and confidently - and with a greater chance of success.

The use of space and movement makes the conversation more focused and builds automatic achievement and feedback into the process.

Roger says: *Back to the Future is loosely based on a scaling exercise that I found in William Cade's "Brief Guide to Brief Therapy". Whenever I see a useful diagram I like to scale it up so that people can walk around inside the diagram. This helps to make great ideas even more powerful. Its therapeutic roots make it great for confidence building, and I have turned it into an exercise that is relevant for anyone who has a goal they want to achieve.*

In the next chapter, you'll find a complementary technique used to overcome a team's limitations and improve its performance.

2.9: ♣ Futures: Missing Person - what kind of newcomer would really benefit this group?

Missing Person is a task in which a team creates an imaginary person who will help the team overcome its limitations and bring about improved team performance. The new character represents the skills, roles and qualities that the team has so far lacked or need in greater measure. This new person can also have characteristics that are already well represented in the group.

I encourage you to start with a briefing in which you ask everyone to think about:

- What kind of new team member would help to improve team performance?
- What qualities would help to make the person accepted as a team member?
- What extra strengths and skills would you like the new person to bring?

Very important! Tell the team to: start with a name (that can be changed later), get drawing early in the process and only use words if the desired qualities cannot be illustrated. Then ask each group to introduce the person they have created while explaining how this person will help to improve teamwork and team performance.

This works well after a few team activities or after the group has worked on a variety of tasks.
If you do it indoors, use flip paper and pens.
Outdoors, the group can scavenge for natural or artificial resources from which to make their missing person (thus creating environmental art). In the outdoor version it is easier for more people to be involved and 'artist's block' does not stop people from gathering and arranging materials.
It usually takes 10 to 15 minutes creating the person, maybe a bit more for the outdoor version.

In order to encourage full participation you should divide large teams into smaller groups of 4 to 7 people, provide plenty of pens and place the paper on table surfaces, flip charts are a pain to draw on.

As I've previously stated, people feel they create or actually do create art so take into consideration the emotional attachment that will come with those drawings. Do not to destroy art works: the creators should dispose of their own creations.

And even if the images are soon forgotten, it is still a valuable review exercise – because the task involves the group considering its strengths, needs, skills and qualities. If the imaginary person 'lives on' after the event, it may assist with learning transfer. On the other hand, the better this exercise has worked, the more likely it is that the team will have learned the lessons and have already moved on.

The power of the created image can be stronger than any action plan, but in some situations an action plan **will add value**. So, as a variation of the method, ask the team **who** will take responsibility for each of the desired changes and for ensuring that they actually happen.

I've personally used a variation to identify the participants' needs in the first day of a leadership training. They created a person that had the qualities they lacked and also the qualities they wanted to promote and maintain in the group. From that we identified together some leadership attributes that were considered lacking and then I developed some games for the next few days that helped express those missing leadership attributes. (Bogdan)

Roger reveals how the Missing Person exercise was born: *I was once a group facilitator on an open enrolment personal development programme and one of the participants never turned up. The group decided to include this missing person in most of their activities. Little by little the character of this person developed and became very much a part of the group and the group's identity despite being totally invisible. The process was so powerful and positive that I sought a way of making it happen more deliberately. That is where the Missing Person comes from.*

Quiz: Bridging past, present and future

1. Back to the Future is an exercise that focuses on helpful factors in the past and present that are real and available for achieving an important goal.
True
False
2. Back to the Future is a short journey in which:

- The '_____' asks the '_____' to reflect on assets that will help them achieve their _____.
- The 'traveller' turns their back to the future in order to focus on helpful factors in the _____ and _____.
- The _____'s questions all use the same format: "What knowledge or skills (or something else) do you _____ have that will help you on this _____?"

Back to the Future is a 'just-in-time' review process that precedes _____. Think of it as an audit of assets, strengths and resources. It is _____ a substitute for making a plan - but it is likely to result in a much better plan.

3. The 'coach' can apply the same questioning process to any problem that the 'traveller' happens to mention: "What ... do you already have that will help you overcome this obstacle?"
True
False

4. In Missing Person the group make a picture of an imaginary team member whose presence would help them work better as a team and achieve a higher level of performance.
True
False

5. What should you encourage people to pay attention to when briefing Missing Person?

When briefing Missing Person encourage the team to start with a thorough analysis of their strengths and weaknesses as a team.

When briefing Missing Person encourage the team to find the best artist before they begin.

When briefing Missing Person encourage the team to: start with a name and to get drawing early in the process only using words if the desired qualities cannot be readily illustrated.

When briefing Missing Person make it a competition to increase motivation.

When briefing Missing Person use plenty of examples from previous courses to illustrate your verbal briefing.

(you can find the answers in the Appendix)

Chapter 3: Implementing ART into your training

3.1: When to review?

Time is of the essence, so...when to review? Below, you have a list of 10 practical tips on how to design a reviewing strategy for experiential learning programs.They are:

1. How to ensure that your programme design protects review time;
2. Why you should schedule your first review as early as possible;
3. Reasons to include a participatory demonstration of active reviewing;
4. Why you should choose the reviewing methods before you choose the activities;
5. The benefits of beginning with the experience in mind;
6. How to design a progressive sequence of review sessions;
7. Why you should work backwards from the start, outwards from the middle and backwards from the end;
8. When and where to place the various activities you'll be implementing;
9. How to provide a holistic experience with Learning Style Preferences; Right Brain, Left Brain; The Combination Lock Model
10. And finally, how to Test and Evaluate your design.

Roger offers further details and explanation of the tips at http://www.activereviewing.com/bonuses .
Download and then keep on reading.

3.2: Not enough time for reviewing?

Have you ever felt the need to shrink activities or reviews?
Are you in general pressured to achieve more in less time?
Have your clients expected the outcomes you once offered in 5-day programmes to be achieved in only 1 or 2 days?
Maybe found yourself speaking quickly to fit more in...?
And last but not least, are you quicker to fill in silence and quicker to explain things in your own words when participants are slow to come up with 'the right answer'?

If you've answered "yes" to all the questions above, then the moment to change that ineffective scenarios has finally come! I know that there is an increasing demand for quick reviews. But experiential learning takes time. Speed is not its selling point. What if instead, you could make reviewing so active and stimulating that the distinction between "activity" and "review"starts to disappear?
Whenever you are short of time for the kind of review that you'd like to offer, I'd advise 2 courses of action:

1) Go for the short-term fix of finding a suitably quick review method
or
2) Go for the long term fix of redesigning your programmes in a way that shows a full understanding

of (and commitment to) the principles of experiential learning.

Be careful!

If your reviewing is too quick, the value of what you are providing starts to crash. Few clients would be dumb enough to accept that a 5-minute review entitles you to double your prices compared to the 'activities-only' provider down the road.

Sometimes pressure for quick reviews (or even no reviews!) comes from participants. My advice to you is not to let this pressure create a vicious cycle in which you are unable to persuade participants of the value of reviewing. Furthermore, do not persuade yourself that all participants love activities and hate reviews - because you would be wrong. Sell them the reviewing process by wrapping it up in a dynamic, fun way and they see how your trainees will happily engage in it.

The challenge for programme designers is to retain the right kind of balance so that participants value review as much as they value activity.

Roger says: "*It was my own evaluations of experiential learning programmes that showed me just how wrong it is to believe that reviewing is unpopular with participants. In these evaluations, mixed ability groups of teenagers from across the social spectrum regularly chose reviewing as the highest point of their programmes. It was in reviews that they felt listened to, respected, supported, treated as responsible people, valued by peers, etc. These were not quick reviews - and I think these young people would have complained if we had reduced review time."*

3.3: What could possibly go wrong? - spot these traps and know how to avoid them

Big fears and little fears can get in the way of learning anything new. So what fears might facilitators have about reviewing - especially facilitators who are new to reviewing? Below you have a list of the most common misbeliefs and their countermeasures:

1. "PARTICIPANTS MAY HAVE NOTHING TO SAY"

Passing is OK. Silence is also OK - especially if it is a reflective silence.
Participants without answers may have questions they want to ask- so ask them if they have questions.
Give learners thinking time, and then, talking time with a partner, and they will be better prepared for speaking up in a large group. Or you can use visual methods where drawings, pictures or objects do some of the 'talking'.

2. "THEY MAY FIND IT BORING"

It is helpful to pitch the review at a suitably challenging level. You can also design the review as a challenging task, such
as by:
- Asking learners to reenact key events or write news reports in the style of certain newspapers or magazines,
- Or by asking subgroups to prepare balanced feedback for each individual in another subgroup.

Tip: Responsibilities within reviews (such as observer, learning buddy, artist and chair) provide challenge and purpose, especially when individuals volunteer for specific responsibilities. Better still, if participants receive appreciative feedback from their peers about how they perform their special responsibility.

3. "IT MAY JUST REPEAT WHAT THEY ALREADY KNOW"

General discussion about the group's performance tend to produce repetition and cliché. So ask for examples that may have gone unnoticed. Or focus the discussion on individual performance. In 'Empathy Test', for example, people find out just how well they know each other's experiences or opinions related to the event being reviewed.

4. "THEY MIGHT FIND IT PERSONAL OR EMBARRASSING"

If that's the case, allow passing and opting out; tell your participants that they can stop the group process if they have
concerns (e.g. by using a symbol or a stop word). This encourages individuals to take responsibility for themselves and for influencing the group's developing code of conduct.

I recommend you be clear about what you want to achieve from a review, and that you want to avoid any discomfort that gets in the way of learning. This communicates sensitivity and support.

5."I MAY LOSE CONTROL"

It is inevitable that you lose some control because you are not a teacher feeding data into the learning process.
The core process is that of learners reflecting on their own experiences. In many cases you will be giving learners the tools to help them explore and learn from their own experiences. The chances are that you already give learners quite a high level of independence and responsibility within the task that you will later review.

Assuming that they can already handle some independence and responsibility during the task, there is really no need or benefit in seizing it all back in the review.

Very important! Be clear with groups when you want the reins, when you want them to take the reins and when you want to share the reins. This way, both you and your learners are more likely to have the amount of control needed in order create a worthwhile review.

6. "A PIG MIGHT WALK IN"
Read the full story in the additional materials at:
http://www.activereviewing.com/bonuses .

3.4: Top 10 tips for reviewing

1. Ask 'What else? What else? What else?'

To get beyond people's initial responses to a question, try asking: What else did you notice? What else were you thinking? What else went well?

2. Ask 'Why? Why? Why?'

To analyse success or failure more deeply just keep asking 'why?'. But this may seem very aggressive. So explain in advance why you will keep asking 'why?'. The responder may stop the process at any point without explanation. This works well as a paired exercise. You can also take the sting out of a why question by asking "I wonder why ...?" or "I am curious/interested/puzzled about why ..." or "What was your motivation at the point when you ...?"

3. Review anywhere anytime

Reviewing 'little and often' is part of the culture in BP-Amoco, Motorola and General Electric. 'After Action Reviews' are embedded into their way of working.
The 'little and often' principle also applies to training programmes. Quick impromptu debriefs can be even more powerful than the scheduled ones. So use both! If there is not the time or space for a whole group review, there might still be sufficient time for a worthwhile review in 2s or 3s.

4. Ask 'What worked well?'

However good or bad the performance, it is good to acknowledge what worked well and trace the causes. Performance improvement comes from studying success as well as from studying failure.

5. Provide notebooks

Learning from experience cannot be recorded in advance! Provide notebooks for recording experiences, ideas and applications.
Provide guidance about note taking and the time to do it well.
For example: make initial notes on left hand pages and save the right hand pages for follow-up actions when re-reading notes.

6. Use review tasks

If participants respond well to tasks but less well to debriefs, then make the debrief a task. The task can be to create a news report or mind map or flowchart or to prepare a demonstration showing what participants would keep and change if doing the same task again.

7. Keep moving

If people always sit in the same seats they can both look and feel stuck. Keep changing the group dynamics, use subgroups, vary the review tasks, change the pace and style. Keep some routines, but you won't break the mould by staying in one!

8. Review the review

You will become better at debriefing if you regularly review your debriefing sessions. So review the reviews as well as the training exercises. Everyone will benefit. Try using a variety of methods to help you reflect on your own practice.

For example: seek the views of participants using Horseshoe; make your own Storyline showing your own ups and downs during the review session - and talk this through with a colleague; co-facilitate and give each other feedback.

9. Use several models

There is no single model that is so superior that it should be followed to the exclusion of others. There are more good ways of learning than can be captured in any single model - just as there is no perfect model for a good conversation. Good learning conversations can be just as varied, open, exploratory and surprising as any other kind of good conversation.

10. Be a model

The most important model is you. Find opportunities to demonstrate that you are learning from experience. Join in some of your own reviewing exercises. Share your own learning goals. Seek feedback at suitable opportunities. Taste some of your own medicine. Also know when it is time to step to one side and give full opportunities for participants to follow your example or find their own ways to learn from experience..

3.5: Q&A: Participation leads to learning. Do you agree?

"Practice makes perfect" is as valid today as it was 100 years ago… But even more so nowadays, with all the gadgets and the media that enable us to refine our skills. We, the trainers, believe in lifelong learning and in the naked truth that everybody makes mistakes. That is why we encourage you to contact us, bug us with questions, give feedback! Feedback has become one of the most valuable units of communication and recognition and we know (and now you know, too) that we "can't live without it".

So don't be shy and contact us personally. We all answer our emails ;)
- Roger Greenaway- roger@reviewing.co.uk
- Călin Iepure- contact@caliniepure.ro
- Bogdan Vaida- office@vaidabogdan.com

Oh, and for our personal motivation as trainers, do leave us a review where you purchased the book from. We love reading them before going to a training (even if they are timely reminders about what *not* to do).

Chapter 4: What's next?

4.1: SURVEY: Help us improve the toolkit

Because we are constantly working on how to improve the quality of our books and courses, we would like you to take the following survey. By completing it, you will offer us valuable information, which will help better address the needs and wants of our students.

Follow this link: http://www.activereviewing.com/help3

4.2: BONUS: Access the video course that this book was based upon

This book is based on the video course that Roger, Călin and I launched on http://www.activereviewing.com .

If you want to get the video version of the methods described in the book, together with visual examples and recordings from our trainings, then forward Bogdan (office@vaidabogdan.com) the proof of payment received when you purchased this book to receive an even better deal for the online version.

PS: Would you like to receive The Active Reviewing Toolkit (a 32 pages PDF detailing all the methods presented in the book with step by step instructions, useful variations and detailed explanations on why, how and when to use them), free book updates and other complementary materials? If so, subscribe here:

http://www.activereviewing.com/bonuses ! You'll get all the bonuses on your email address, fast and easy!

4.3: BONUS: How to sell a training

"What? I? Sell? But I'm just a trainer... I only know how to facilitate learning for groups... I only know how a presentation is done... and if I think about it, in the end, I'm not the one who should be selling the training... Others should! In fact, I'm so good at what I do that the trainings will sell themselves!"
I wonder how many of us trainers can relate to the statements above, at least to a part of it, anyway. Unfortunately, when people hear the word "selling", they often become reluctant; they tend to draw back because it requires of them an ability they do not possess. Which is a shame...? Why? Well, Brian Tracy says that „You could be only one skill away from doubling your income". Hmmm, now that sounds good doesn't it?
Your duty becomes now to identify that specific lacking skill and then concentrate on developing it. And if this ability can lead to success is one and the same with the „ability to sell" your trainings and workshops, well, why not go for it and do it?
This article contains insight from my personal experience with selling educational courses to companies- small, big and even national ones. What I'm sharing is the principles behind the process, because trust me, they're the same no matter what level the players are on!

1. Researching target market, defining client profile and sparking curiosity

"Not all clients are the right ones for me!" and "Not all clients are the same!" are two statements that are important to bear in mind when it comes to researching target market.

And it's *because* **not all clients are the same** and *because* **clients' needs can differ** in terms of work field, size of portfolio, geographic area where they operate, etc., that you thoroughly need to research the market before diving in.

To plan out doesn't just mean you're making a list with the names and addresses of potential clients. Your organization should include much more, like for instance:

§ First, clearly establish what's your client's profile (or avatar)

§ Secondly, find out as much as possible about potential needs/problems they are having at the moment

Example:

Client profile	Potential needs / problems
Medium-size IT company (50-100 employees)	Bad communication within programming teams Bad communication between departments

Once you've defined the basic needs, the next step is to spark your client's curiosity about what you can offer, i.e. your services. If you are unable to do that, the transaction is basically over. That would be very bad for you, as *first impression is essential in business.* I'm sure you know the saying "dress to impress", but here it's with a different spin: **"Plan to impress!"**.

Example:

Client profile	How to spark curiosity
Medium-size IT company (50-100 employees)	Hold a communications training at an IT conference. Something entitled like: "Communicate efficiently! How to double your team's productivity through communication" [or] Organize an OPEN training (maybe for free) to which you can invite companies that match the desired profile [or] Take part in HR specialists meetings (there you can find IT company representatives and network with them)

2. Building a relationship and gauging your client

It's said our ability to set up good relationships depends a great deal on how well our first contact goes. A study done by Dr. Leonard Zunin in the US shows that connection with the receiver of your message is established, reconfirmed (in the case of an older acquaintance) or rejected within *the first 4 minutes*.

Therefore, a positive first impression can determine a long-lasting relationship or the start of a pleasant conversation. It's important to know how to get your client on the same page from the very start!

Here you have 3 methods to help you achieve that:
o Dress the same whey they do. Apparel takes up to 90% of the impact of a first impression. Sometimes,

you can take a chance and wear a "Whatzit" (any unusual object that draws attention and helps break the ice)

o Sit straight. Nonverbal communication is crucial during a business meeting as it indirectly feeds information about your confidence, status and overall skills. So remember, keep your back straight and your shoulders back!

o Smile. When you smile, you're subconsciously saying "I am friendly and I'm open", which is an invitation to dialogue.

Other methods involve using a customized business card and high-quality handouts.

Client profile	How to create a first good impression
Medium-size IT company (50-100 employees)	I dress like the company's representative I have a positive attitude that shows confidence I smile and sit straight

This is also the time to gauge you client, in other words, assess whether they fit the profile you are looking for. It's only natural that not any company that you contact (and which you have a good working relation with) is a company that will go along with the purchase of the training. Keep in mind that an organization has priorities of its own and rules it must follow so it can be able to address the management for educational courses.

Client evaluation is a high objective for any trainer who plans to make a successful deal; if the customer meets all the necessary criteria, it will be able to access the training and if not, it won't mean a waste of time on both sides. Disregarding this aspect will bring about a misuse of valuable resources and a potentially negative output.

3. Establishing needs

This stage can be difficult for both trainer (who must know what and when to ask questions) and the client company (because it should answer the questions in a clear and detailed fashion).
My experience so far has led me to situations that usually present themselves with inherent obstacles such as

1. The trainer is in a rush to get the job over with and skips this step altogether because of a preconceived idea he/she knows the client's needs best

2. The client company's representative rushes (or skips) this step so that employees don't lose valuable work time
If the definition of "to need" is "to want, to require", then from a trainer's perspective, the client's need is to solve an important problem or prevent an impactful problem from appearing in the near future. All of this being handled of course, without exceeding the budget.

A trainer always has to check if there's a real training need by thoroughly researching the customer and making sure all the necessary characteristics for pitching sell are met.
Many times, a clear analysis leads to identifying secondary needs and that in its turn can set the foundation for a long term partnership.

Client profile	How to establish needs
Medium-size IT company (50-100 employees)	Ask the manager questions Ask the employees around Take notes on behavior Have a meeting with involved parties ....

4. Presentation of the training and the (perfect) solution

Extremely important! This step must take place during a different scheduled meeting.

Well, this looks like an easy and applicable thing to do! It's not...
The difficulty consists in the following:
o Finding and using a language that bridges communication with the client no matter how complex the training or service solution you're offering is. It's now appropriate to use the relaxing technique "This reminds me of...";
o Giving the whole picture, not only the main features. Focus on listing the benefits of the deal you're trying to sell them on. Don't forget to mention the amazing results your training course will bring about because most often, the client is more interested in the endgame.

Client profile	How to sell the solution/training course
Medium-size IT company	Use an easy-to-understand language Use the "This reminds me of the..."

(50-100 employees)	technique Present the training's main features Highlight the benefits and the results (abilities, behavior, etc.) ....

Of course, there is also the part in which the customer asks for something you can't give. You know what to do, right...? Well, you should!

5. Overcoming a huge obstacle- objections

Many people believe that during this stage, they should use an entire arsenal of manipulation techniques designed to persuade the buyer of the fact that his/her objection has no foothold in reality. Good luck with that, because this point of view is fundamentally wrong!

Please keep in mind that 90% of the objections voiced afterwards come from a faulty presentation.

The trainer's difficulty in facing and fencing disagreements comes more likely from a rush to immediately answer an objection (maybe stemming from a desire to show promptness or availability), rather than taking the proper time to analyze it clearly and see whether there is any real concern.
Truth be told, any clear, solid objection carries an underlying request that the training service *can* or *cannot* comply with. That's all!
In the end, even if the client wants something that the course doesn't have, the sell isn't truly lost! The

trainer will just have to walk the extra mile to deliver it...

6. Negotiating and sealing the deal

The most important step of the selling process is represented by negotiation and then sealing the deal. Here is some advice worth following when you're aiming to close a sell:

o Clearly determine what you want to negotiate (Ex: the training's modules, the price, number of participants, duration, guarantee, etc.)

o Set up clear standards for yourself (Ex: the course shouldn't under any circumstance take less than 2 days)

o Willingness to compromise (Ex: if I add an extra module, what do I get from you?)

o Getting confirmation, ending negotiations and agreeing to final contract terms

7. References and keeping in touch

Once the training is over, it's worth contacting your client and even paying him a visit. This way you can get valuable feedback that will help figure out what to improve in the future and when approached again for a new contract, you'll get it done in half the time!

An old saying goes "Birds of a feather flock together"; so why not apply this to business? I recommend exploring your customer's partners because if you deliver good results, word will spread and you might end up in a meeting room right across the building you first pitched a sell just a little while ago! Here is yet another reason why you should network.

Also, use the internet- search for people you've chatted with via LinkedIn and take a look at their connections. Analyze them and see if you can be recommended to new potential clients.

By precisely following the steps described above, you will raise efficiency and your chances of closing a transaction more quickly, whether we're talking about selling a training or a connected service. Moreover, your success will come once you are completely focused on your clients' situation and the improvement of the company you own.

4.4: BONUS: The 6 steps in building a successful training

In the following guide you'll find the ingredients for a successful training; this recipe applies directly to business trainings, but it can be adapted to open-type courses, as well.
For a training to be impactful, it must adhere to the basic elements of any efficient project: setting up objectives, the process itself and evaluation.

The objectives setup starts with an analysis of the client's needs, which will then lead to establishing proper goals. **The process** entails the creation of a lesson plan, based primarily on the adult learning theory, a selection of the best training methods and the approach that will emphasize facilitation techniques. By **evaluation** one will understand the quality assessment of the delivered educational course, as well as the assessment of potentially improvable aspects.

STEP 1. Assessing the client's needs

A successful training starts with identifying the needs of the participants. Their current behavior is observed to establish how the participants usually do things, in contrast to the way things should be done (this process is called the GAP process).

This analysis is normally done through observation, by asking questions, by having an interview with all stakeholders or a combination of the three.

As you can see, new information is gathered regarding what skills and behaviors need to be changed. Once that is completed, the specific objectives of the training are set.

STEP 2. Establishing training objectives

This phase is about turning the performance deficiencies identified in Step 1 into real, solid objectives.

The following questions pops up: How does one efficiently formulate an objective?

A training is defined by a sentence formulated from the participant's point of view; for it to work, it has to be oriented toward action. Remember, an objective that doesn't stimulate action (participation) is pretty much worthless.

It's best if the objective contains the phrasing "You will be able to…" also, the more specific and detailed it is, the more realistic it is going to get. Let me give you an example:

for a training entitled "How to negotiate like pro", a possible objective might sound something like this: "At the end of this training you will have found the 3 decisive questions one should answer before initiating any negotiation".

To make things easier, look at the table below and follow my lead. Once you've set all the objectives, fill in the time that you think will be best allocated for the course, then move on to completing the necessary equipment (laptop, flipchart, markers, etc.), and last but not least, the audience you are addressing.

Training plan draft (lesson plan)

Title:

Objective: At the end of this course you will be able to...

Necessary time/Allocated time:

Location:

Necessary equipment:

Targeted audience:

STEP 3: Creating a lesson plan based on the adult learning theory

The role of a trainer is different from the one of a teacher's because of the way adults assimilate. There is a notable difference between children and adults; with children, you decide what's important, but with adults that rapport doesn't exist as they are the ones who decide what's relevant for them. The key word here is *autonomy*.

At the same time, children do not possess experience they can share, while adults can be stimulated to participate and infuse the learning process with valuable, personal input. A good trainer will use the shared experience and integrate it in the training.

Dr. Malcolm Knowles, an authority in the domain, developed 4 principles that should be included in the course you wish to create.

They are:
1. Adults must be involved in planning the process and be then able to correlate learning to their own goals
2. The content and the participants' experience should correspond as much as possible
3. Adults are motivated to learn when they identify a need to do so
4. Adults look for logical answers to their problems

So once you've defined the objectives, it's necessary that you group them in logic sequences or draft a plan; that will make the outline of the presentation. Here's an example:

Fragment from the "How to negotiate like a pro" training	
NO	**SUBJECT**
1.	Introducing the trainer and communicating the
2.	Introduction in Negotiation
3.	Business meeting simulation

4.	......

STEP 4: Choosing training methods

A frequent training method is knowledge transfer from the trainer to the trainee. There are many training methods out there such as "Presentation", „Role-play", "Exercises'", "Case studies", "Demos", "Questions round" and others.
This article will focus on: presentation and role-playing.

Presentation

Just as the name suggests, a presentation is a planned speech. In fact, it's the most used method in the book and unfortunately, many young novice trainers abuse it. However, in order to make the presentation more interesting (if you still want to go for this method and are one to chat much) you CAN:
1.   Boil it down to 15 min max
2.   Use visual aids
3.   Engage with the public by asking confirmation questions like "How many of you have been in a negotiation at least once this year? Raise your hand if you have.

Role-play

… enables the participants to integrate learnt content more easily by simulating real-life situations.

Every participant is given a role and a situation they must enact. It is recommendable to have an observer who takes notes, so at the end there can be a fruitful dialogue between all the members of your group. Role-play is a valuable tool that gives the trainees the chance to practice what they've learnt or, to determine what stage of the learning process they are in.

Of course, for impact and success, you should vary training methods every 15 minutes and most definitely adapt them to the typologies of the people present in the room. Don't forget to also add necessary materials in the plan. Take a look at the table below to get a better picture!

Fragment from the "How to negotiate like a pro" training			
TIME	**SUBJECT**	**TRAINING METHOD**	**MATERIALS**
15 min	Introducing the trainer and communicating the agenda	Presentation	Laptop Projector PPT Slideshows
3 min	Introduction in Negotiation	Video	DVD Video
15 min	Business meeting	Role-play	2 chairs

	simulation		a table
...	....	...	...

STEP 5: Implementing facilitation techniques

This is actually the most important step of all! Even though you've thoroughly planned your training needs in advance, have developed the plan, have chosen the appropriate methods for this course, your responsibility as a trainer doesn't end here! It's essential to fully understand the facilitation techniques needed so that you can interact with the group as best as possible.
As a result, if you use "asking questions" and "giving feedback" during the course, you will be able to create the ideal learning environment.

Questions

By asking questions you stimulate participation and interaction. This motivates your audience to listen more closely and be even more involved in the process.
As trainer, you can opt for one or more of the following types of questions:

o **Direct questions** – addressed to a particular participant, in order to draw attention (Ex: How has this method worked for you, John?)
o **Questions directed to the whole group** – to stimulate dialogue (Ex: Why is it worth it to learn

communication techniques when we're talking about negotiation?)

o **Open questions** – scouts opinions (Ex: How would you apply this?)

o **Closed questions** – they're fast and useful when feedback from a trainee is needed (Ex: Is this principle relevant for you?)

As you can see, it's important to formulate your questions clearly so that they are easy to understand.

Feedback

According to Merriam-Webster's Online Dictionary, the word *feedback* was first used in electronics and meant "the return to the input of a part of the output of a machine, system, or process…" and so on and so forth. In translation plus an example, feedback explains how a thermostat makes the *necessary changes* according to air temperature. But how is this relevant to you?

Well, during a course, the trainer gives the participants feedback throughout its duration so that the trainees can assimilate the information more easily. Feedback is used by the participants and it allows them to interpret behavior and understand how this impacts people around them.

There are several aspects that should be taken into consideration when offering feedback, as it can sometimes be a delicate process:

1. Don't get into too much detail
2. Focus more on behavior, rather than on the person
3. Don't delay giving feedback
4. Be tactful with your choice of words
5. Communicate clearly and check if you've been understood

An efficient feedback phrasing you could use is (see below):

I liked... (behavior).
My advice to you is/My suggestion is... (an improvement suggestion clearly formulated),
...because this will help with... (what achievement the trainee can obtain).

STEP 6: Evaluating a training course

No matter how good a course is, there will always be room for improvement. In order to determine what aspects should be made better, a questionnaire at the end of the training is a simple and effective way to find out.
Of course, there are guidelines for a good form, too! Look at the questions below for a more specific view:

Questions about the training

1. Were the objectives clearly expressed?
2. Were the objectives accessible and measurable?
3. Was the adult learning theory taken into consideration?
4. Were the auxiliary materials useful for the participants?
5. Was the lesson plan well-structured?
6. Were the activities pertaining to the course (objectives)?

Questions about the trainer

1. What part of the presentation did you like best?
2. Was the trainer well-trained?

3. Did the visual aids help you understand the content better?
4. How comprehensive was the trainer's presentation?

Questions about the participants

Participants' impressions are important because they help you see how you are perceived as a trainer. For that, I encourage you to ask OPEN questions, like so:

1. How did you feel when you took part in the exercises?
2. How would you estimate different sections of the course?
3. What improvements would you make?

Certainly, results speak louder than anything else. On that note, here are some clear-cut questions:

1. What will you apply starting tomorrow?
2. What is the most valuable piece of information to you?

If the feedback is positive, you can hold the training again without any minor fixes. But if it's negative, it's worth spending time improving or even designing a new one.

Training is serious business!

It's true, it does take a lot of time and effort to plan a course that's excellent; but by carefully going through all 6 steps, you will be able to create a wonderful material, indeed.

One thing, though... don't forget to wrap your content in those unforgettable and unique experiences in order to bring extra value to your training! The experiences can only be created with the help of advanced facilitation techniques.

4.5: Final words - your next steps can ensure that your own learning becomes active

The most important part of the training happens after the training is over.

That's the moment when you decide to dismiss it from your mind.. or put it to practice.

Question:
How many true athletes would say: "I've trained, I'm in great condition, but I don't think I'm going to race. Why bother?" ?
The answer:
None.

Question:
How many real playwrights would say: "The final act doesn't really matter"?
The answer:
None.

The point is that talent, opportunity and the right circumstances should never be wasted! And by "wasting", we also understand letting dust settle over newly-acquired skills, no matter what domain we're talking about. So, if you took part in a training course that had enriched you (at least) content-wise, wouldn't you use it? We encourage our students to implement the methods and techniques provided by this book so that at the end of the day, they have truly done something productive.

Don't let this book be your last experience with Active Reviewing!
Check your calendar. When's your next training?
Let's add to it 2 of the methods you've just learned.
How about.. Horseshoe? Aaaand.. Empathy Test?
2 easy to learn, easy to implement methods.

I, Călin and most of the participants from our last training with Roger have already implemented the methods he has taught us. And we're not the only ones. After facilitating a public speaking session in Slovenia, a leader from an Armenian non-profit organization came to me and said that she'd learned so much from the public speaking part... but not so much during the exercises per se, rather from the reflection time taken by students, at the end of the learning session. She told me she would implement these reviewing techniques into her own trainings around the world.

You have already come a long way in understanding how active reviewing works and what's more, you have acquired the necessary know-how to implement it in the real world.

Now it's time for action! Train people you will, little padawan! May the force be with you!

Use the techniques you've learned here in your trainings but don't stop there!

Modify them; improve on them so that they best fit your trainer personality.

And if you have a suggestion for future improvement, don't forget to leave us a comment with the new version.
We'd love hearing from you and would greatly appreciate any variation that enhances the participant's learning experience.

Thank you for taking the time to go through this book and.. see you in our next one :)

Appendix: Quiz answers

Quiz: Reviewing with playing cards

1. diamonds, feelings, spades, futures, Joker
2. True
3. True
4. a)
5. b)

Teachable moments:

4.a. Yes - this is least likely to be a Clubs (future-oriented) question because it refers exclusively to the past. This is a good example of a question to ask in the Diamonds zone.

4.b. This is a future-oriented question so it belongs in clubs. (It is also asking for a demonstration - making it an "active reviewing" question.)

4.c. This is a future-oriented question so it belongs in clubs. (It is an invitation to do something which makes it an "active reviewing" question.)

4.d. This is a future-oriented question so it belongs in clubs. (It also clearly refers to the past which is good practice because in the futures/clubs zone it is often helpful to build links between past and future.)

4.e. This is a future-oriented question so it belongs in clubs. (The use of visual aids by participants is also an example of "active reviewing".)

5.a. A joker is a fun person, but in this model the Joker Card is a wild card that can be anything.

5.b. Precisely! The Joker Card can represent anything.

5.c. Not a bad answer, but the Joker is not limited to any particular method such as asking questions
5.d. Possibly. It could equally come after any of the other three cards. Or it can even exist independently without any connection to the other cards.

Quiz: Working with facts and first assumptions

1. e)
2. True
3. True
4. Action Replay can create useful videos to assist with learning transfer.
5. dummy, pause, interview, cycle

Teachable moments:

1.a. This is a likely outcome.
1.b. This is a likely outcome.
1.c. This is a likely outcome.
1.d. This is a likely outcome.
1.e. This is the most unlikely outcome. Participants may happen to learn how to make this very specific kind of map - but this has very little to do with the making of any other kind of map.
4.a. This is a likely outcome from Action Replay.
4.b. This is a likely outcome from Action Replay but maybe not everyone gets to perform or gets to feel good about their performance.
4.c. This is the most unlikely result because the kind of Action Replay that we describe in this course does not involve the use of video technology (even if this 'least likely' answer has sparked a good idea).
4.d. This is a likely outcome from Action Replay.
4.e. This is a likely outcome from Action Replay.

Quiz: Focusing on feelings and experiences

1. Empathy Test can be useful for Training Needs Analysis
2. True
3. True
4. Storyline works best for people who have high emotional intelligence.
5. True

Teachable moments:

1.a. Yes: this statement is least likely to apply to Empathy Test. The word "Test" does suggest that you get test results - but these are only of passing value and have no validity beyond the context of this empathy-developing game.
1.b. True, but you are looking for a statement that does not apply. Questions about feelings are an obvious place to start (which is why Empathy Test "belongs" in hearts), but asking people to think what their partner is thinking involves some degree of empathy.
1.c. True, but you are looking for a statement that does not apply.
1.d. True, but you are looking for a statement that does not apply.
1.e. True, but you are looking for a statement that does not apply. If the pairings are random it becomes a pure guessing game, rather than being a game draws on observation, intuition and shared experiences.

4.a. This is true, but you are looking for a misrepresentation of Storyline.

4.b. This is true, but you are looking for a misrepresentation of Storyline.
4.c. This is a misrepresentation for the following reasons: a mobility aid does not "work best" for people with high mobility (Storyline is a storytelling aid); Storyline is not limited to emotional stories (even though it is clearly good for that purpose); Storyline can be of value at many levels.
4.d. This is true, but you are looking for a misrepresentation of Storyline.
4.e. This is true, but you are looking for a misrepresentation of Storyline.

Quiz: Digging deeper and finding out

1. False
2. True
3. statements, straight, curved, stand, eye, facilitating
4. You can readily assess participants by observing the positions they choose.
5. True

Teachable moments:

4.a. This is a very likely outcome from Horseshoe.
4.b. This is a very likely outcome from Horseshoe.
4.c. This is a very likely outcome from Horseshoe.
4.d. This is a possible outcome from using Horseshoe, but if you use Horseshoe for assessing individuals your chances of achieving the other benefits are likely to fade away.
4.e. This is a very likely outcome from Horseshoe.

Quiz: Bridging past, present and future

1. True
2. coach, traveller, goal; past, present; coach, already, journey; planning, not
3. True
4. True
5. When briefing Missing Person encourage the team to: start with a name and to get drawing early in the process only using words if the desired qualities cannot be readily illustrated.

Teachable moments:

5.a. This is not the best answer because Missing Person is designed to access both creative and logical thinking and provides a balanced and inspirational alternative to an over-analytical approach.

5.b. This is not the best answer because Missing Person should be presented in a way that encourages full participation from all team members - it is not an art competition. And expecting one person to do all the work is not in the spirit of teamwork.

5.c. This is the best answer because it emphasises the creative aspects of this method while recognising some limitations of a purely creative process.

5.d. This is not a good answer because making this method competitive can distort motivation, can create demotivation among losers, and does little to encourage attentive listening and appreciation.

5.e. This is not the best answer because presenting model answers for Missing Person can lead to copying rather than creativity, can make participants more outward looking at a time when you want them to be more inward looking and can make participants think that the quality of the image is the top priority.

CPSIA information can be obtained
at www.ICGtesting.com
Printed in the USA
LVOW13s1046020117
519424LV00008BA/571/P

9 781519 392336